AF421348

Beneath The Chinar Trees

A Timeless Tales Collection

SYED MUSTAHSAN

TIMELESS
TALES
@tales.timeless_

@tales.
timeless_

For the heartbroken yet brave souls who continue to love fiercely, find strength in vulnerability, and courage in the face of adversity. Your resilience inspires us all.

Foreword

In the heart of the Kashmir Valley, where nature weaves tales as intricate as its landscapes, **Beneath the Chinar Trees** unfolds a poignant narrative of love, loss, and the inexorable passage of time. As we journey through the lives of Zain and Amina, we are invited to explore not just the breathtaking beauty of Dal Lake or the ancient chinar trees that stand sentinel over their memories, but the profound emotional landscapes that shape their destinies.

The story begins with Zain, whose life is steeped in the serene yet tumultuous backdrop of Srinagar. The early morning mist over Dal Lake mirrors the unfinished promises of his past, particularly the haunting memory of Amina, a spirited soul whose dreams and aspirations extend beyond the borders of their beloved valley. Their love blossoms amidst the political unrest that surrounds them, encapsulating the hopes and fears of a generation yearning for freedom.

Each chapter peels back layers of their relationship, revealing the complexities of longing and the painful choices that life sometimes demands. Amina's departure is not just a physical absence; it marks a deep emotional void that Zain struggles to fill. The harsh realities of their homeland where beauty and conflict coexist serve as a powerful backdrop, reminding us that the heartache of separation is often inextricably linked to the landscapes we cherish.

As Zain navigates his life without Amina, the narrative elegantly transitions from the tenderness of young love to the silence that follows in her absence. It is a silence punctuated by memories and the weight of unspoken words. Yet, beneath this silence lies the hope that love can endure even the most formidable obstacles.

The return of Amina in the story's climax serves as a testament to the enduring nature of love. Their reunion beneath the same chinar tree that witnessed their first moments together becomes a powerful symbol of reconciliation not only with each other but also with their shared past and the haunting echoes of their homeland.

Through lyrical prose and rich imagery, the author captures the essence of Kashmira land of beauty that is both a sanctuary and a battleground. **Beneath the Chinar Trees** is more than a love story; it is an exploration of identity, belonging, and the intricate tapestry of human emotions that bind us to our roots, even as we reach for the stars.

As you delve into this remarkable tale, may you find reflections of your own heart and a deeper understanding of the ties that bind us all to the places we call home.

Syed Mustahsan.

Preface

The valley of Kashmir, often referred to as "Paradise on Earth," is a place of enchanting beauty and deep rooted cultural heritage. It is a land where the snowcapped mountains kiss the skies, where the lush gardens bloom in vibrant colours, and where the serene waters of Dal Lake reflect the timeless charm of its surroundings. Yet, beneath this idyllic exterior lies a complex tapestry of human experience blend of love, pain, hope, and resilience. **Beneath the Chinar Trees** seeks to capture this intricate interplay, exploring the lives of two individuals, Zain and Amina, against the backdrop of their beloved homeland.

As the author, I have always been fascinated by the profound impact that a landscape can have on the human spirit. The chinar trees, with their sprawling branches and vibrant autumn leaves, symbolize not only the beauty of nature but also the strength and endurance of love amidst adversity. They stand witness to the joys and sorrows of those who seek refuge beneath their canopy, providing a space for reflection and connection. It is within this sacred space that Zain and Amina's story unfolds, echoing the timeless themes of longing, loss, and the quest for identity.

This novel is an homage to the resilience of the Kashmiri people and their unwavering spirit in the face of hardship. It is a narrative woven from the threads of personal experiences and historical realities, capturing the essence of a generation caught between the yearning for freedom and the weight of tradition. Through Zain's journey, we are reminded that love is not just a fleeting emotion but a powerful force that shapes our lives and defines our choices.

Writing this book has been both a labour of love and a journey of self discovery. It has allowed me to explore the depths of human connection and the bittersweet nature of memories that linger long after the moment has passed. My hope is that as you turn the pages, you will feel the warmth of the sun setting over the valley, hear the whispers of the wind through the chinar leaves, and experience the emotional ebb and flow that defines Zain and Amina's relationship.

In sharing this story, I invite you to immerse yourself in the rich tapestry of Kashmir's culture and the complexities of its people. May you find, within these pages, reflections of your own journey and a renewed appreciation for the love that transcends boundaries, both geographical and emotional.

Thank you for joining me on this journey.

 Syed Mustahsan.

1. The Silence of Dal.

The early morning mist clung to the surface of Dal Lake like an unfinished promise. From a distance, the silhouettes of shikaras glided silently, their oars slicing through the calm waters. Zain sat on the edge of the wooden pier, watching as the houseboats slowly came to life, their windows aglow with the warmth of dawn. His eyes were fixed on the horizon, but his thoughts were far from the beauty around him. In this serene landscape, all he could feel was the ache of what had once been.

Srinagar, with its centuries old charm, had always been home to Zain. Born and raised in the heart of the city, he had once believed the beauty of the valley mirrored the simplicity of his life. But as he stared across the lake, the mountains in the distance shrouded in fog, he could only think of her Amina.

They had first met under the shade of an ancient chinar tree, in the courtyard of the university, where the branches stretched wide like the arms of history itself. Zain had been studying literature, while Amina was pursuing sociology, fascinated by the stories and struggles of their people. She had always been different not just because of her intellect, but because of the quiet strength she carried, a strength that seemed to anchor him in ways he could never quite explain.

Amina had walked into his life like the first snowfall of winter gentle but unmistakable. They had spent hours by the Jhelum River, talking about poetry, politics, and the future. She had a way of seeing the world that made Zain want to hold on to every word she said. And in those moments, it was easy to believe that the world beyond Kashmir, with all its uncertainties and shadows, could never touch them.

But it had. It always did.

2. A Love Written in Snow.

The first time Zain realized he loved Amina, they were walking through the snow covered streets of old Srinagar. The city was blanketed in white, the rooftops heavy with the weight of winter. The cold air made their breaths visible, mingling in the space between them like whispered confessions.

Amina had looked up at the falling snowflakes, her face radiant under the dim light of a streetlamp. "Do you ever think about leaving?" she had asked, her voice barely audible over the quiet of the night.

Zain had frowned, confused. "Leaving?"

"Kashmir," she said, her breath turning into a misty cloud. "Sometimes I think... maybe we'd be happier somewhere else. Somewhere far away from all of this."

He had never thought about leaving. How could he? The valley was in his blood, its rivers flowing through his veins. But Amina's eyes held something more longing that frightened him.

"Would you really want to leave?" he had asked, though he already knew the answer.

Amina's silence had spoken louder than words.

For a time, they pretended everything was fine. They still met beneath the chinar trees, still talked about the books they read and the future they dreamed of. But something had shifted, like the first crack in the ice. Zain had seen it coming, but like all things inevitable, he had refused to accept it.

3. Shadows of Conflict.

As the years passed, the political unrest in Kashmir grew, casting a shadow over their lives. Protests filled the streets, and the sounds of gunfire and tear gas became part of the everyday rhythm of Srinagar. Zain found solace in his books, in the poetry of Faiz and the verses of Ghalib. But Amina had grown restless. The conflict was suffocating her, and the walls of the valley felt more like a cage with each passing day.

"I can't stay here, Zain," she had said one evening, her voice shaking as they sat by the Dal Lake. "I can't breathe in this place anymore."

Zain had reached for her hand, but she had pulled away, her eyes filled with a mixture of sorrow and frustration. He had always known she was meant for more than what Kashmir could offer, but the thought of her leaving had felt like losing a part of himself.

"Where will you go?" he had asked, though he already knew the answer.

"Delhi, maybe. Or even abroad. There's a world outside this valley, Zain. A world where I don't have to look over my shoulder all the time. A world where I can be free."

He had wanted to ask her to stay. But Zain had never

been selfish, not with Amina. He had always known that her heart was bigger than the confines of their small world.

She had left three months later, her departure marked not by a grand farewell, but by a quiet drive to the airport in the early hours of the morning. Zain had stood in the cold, watching as her taxi disappeared down the road, his heart heavy with the weight of words unsaid.

4. The Long Silence.

Years passed, and the world changed around him.
Srinagar's streets saw moments of peace, punctuated by
bursts of violence that made the quiet all the more
fragile. Zain stayed behind, choosing to teach at the local
college, trying to find meaning in the stories of others
when his own seemed to have come to a standstill.

Amina's absence became part of the landscape of his life,
like the mountains that framed the horizon always there,
always out of reach. Occasionally, he would hear news
of her through mutual friends. She had gone to Delhi,
then to London for her PhD, her research focused on the
displacement of Kashmiri communities. She was doing
well, they said. But she never wrote, and Zain never
called.

He tried to move on. There were other women who were
kind, beautiful, and worthy of love but none who could
fill the space Amina had left behind. He had come to
realize that some absences are permanent, and some
loves are lost not to time, but to circumstance.

5. Beneath the Same Sky.

It was a late autumn evening when Zain received the letter. The envelope was simple, with a London postmark. His hands trembled as he opened it, the weight of the years pressing down on him as he unfolded the single sheet of paper.

"Dear Zain,

I don't know if this letter will ever reach you. I don't know if you've moved on or if you even think of me anymore. But I wanted you to know never forgot. Not you, not us, not Kashmir.

I've spent years trying to find my place in this world, and in all that time, I've realized something: no matter how far I go, I will always carry the valley with me. And I will always carry you.

I'm coming back. Maybe not to stay, but to visit. I hope we can meet.

With love,
Amina"

Zain stared at the letter, the words blurring as his vision clouded with unshed tears. He looked up at the mountains, their peaks now tinged with the golden light of dusk. Somewhere beneath the same sky, Amina was coming home.

And for the first time in years, Zain allowed himself to hope.

6. The Return.

Weeks passed, and winter began to settle over the valley. The first snowfall had just begun, dusting the city in white. Zain stood beneath the same chinar tree where it had all begun, watching as the snowflakes fell silently around him. His heart raced with anticipation, a feeling he hadn't known in years.

In the distance, he saw her Amina, wrapped in a woollen shawl, her face lit by the soft glow of the streetlamp. She stopped a few feet away, her breath visible in the cold air, just as it had been all those years ago.

For a moment, they simply stood there, the weight of their past hanging between them like the winter air. Then, without a word, Zain took a step forward, and Amina smiled smile that carried the warmth of a thousand forgotten summers.

The past could not be changed, but here, beneath the chinar trees, perhaps they could find a way to begin again.

7. A Fragile Hope.

As spring unfolded over the Kashmir Valley, the air was filled with the scent of blooming flowers, a stark contrast to the heaviness that had settled in Zain's heart. Although Amina's return had rekindled a flicker of hope, the shadows of their past loomed large. They spent their days wandering the winding streets of Srinagar, but with each shared laugh, Zain felt the weight of impending loss pressing down on him, a constant reminder that their happiness might be fleeting.

Amina poured herself into her work, striving to make a difference in the lives of the displaced Kashmiri people. She organized community meetings, helping families tell their stories and advocating for their rights. Yet, beneath her passionate exterior, Zain sensed an unshakeable sadness that she tried to mask.

One evening, as they sat by the Dal Lake, the sun dipping below the horizon, Amina turned to Zain, her eyes glistening with unshed tears. "Sometimes, I feel like the valley is calling me back, like it wants to pull me into its depths," she confessed, her voice trembling. "What if this is just a fleeting moment of joy before it all comes crashing down?"

Zain took her hand, trying to reassure her. "We'll face whatever comes together, Amina. We've already fought so much. You have to believe that we can find a way through this."

But Amina's silence spoke volumes. In the depths of her heart, she harboured a fear that no amount of love could banish fear that their happiness was merely a pause in the chaos that surrounded them.

8. The Unravelling.

Weeks turned into months, and the tension in the valley escalated. Protests erupted again, bringing with them the sounds of conflict that had become all too familiar. Zain found himself torn between his love for Amina and the growing unrest that threatened their fragile peace.

One fateful day, while Amina was attending a rally advocating for the rights of the displaced, the situation spiralled out of control. Zain received a frantic phone call from a friend, urging him to come quickly. Heart racing, he rushed to the site, praying that she was safe.

When he arrived, chaos reigned. People were screaming, and the air was thick with smoke and fear. In the midst of the turmoil, Zain spotted Amina, standing her ground, advocating for the voices that had long been silenced. But just as he reached for her, a deafening explosion shattered the air.

Time seemed to freeze as he watched Amina fall to the ground, clutching her chest, her eyes wide with shock. Zain's world came crashing down as he rushed to her side, cradling her in his arms. "Amina, please, stay with me!" he begged, his voice breaking as he felt her warmth fading.

9. The Aftermath.

Days turned into a blur of grief and despair. Amina was gone, taken too soon by the violence that surrounded them. Zain was left shattered, his heart a hollow echo of what it once was. The vibrant world of Kashmir, once filled with beauty and promise, now felt like a cruel reminder of his loss.

He withdrew into himself, haunted by memories of Amina's laughter and the warmth of her touch. Friends reached out, but their words fell on deaf ears. He wandered the streets of Srinagar like a ghost, the colours around him dull and lifeless. The once familiar paths felt foreign, each corner echoing with the pain of her absence.

In his sorrow, Zain sought refuge beneath the chinar trees where they had shared their dreams. The leaves whispered secrets of a past he could no longer grasp. He spent hours there, lost in a fog of memories, speaking to Amina as if she could hear him.

10. The Breaking Point.

As the seasons changed, so did Zain. He stopped teaching, abandoned his friends, and retreated into a world of solitude. Nights were filled with shadows that danced in the corners of his mind, and days blurred into one another as he succumbed to despair.

His mental state began to unravel, slipping into a darkness that was suffocating. He would sit for hours by the lake, staring into the water, hoping to find solace in its depths. Friends noticed his absence and growing instability, but Zain was unreachable, lost in a labyrinth of grief that he could not escape.

One stormy night, as rain poured relentlessly over the valley, Zain stood by the edge of the lake. The world around him roared with thunder, mirroring the turmoil within. In that moment, he felt a sudden pull yearning to join Amina, to escape the unbearable pain of living without her.

With tears streaming down his face, he stepped closer to the water, whispering her name, believing that somehow she could guide him back to her. And as the rain washed over him, he let go of the last remnants of his strength, plunging into the depths of the lake, surrendering to the darkness.

Epilogue: A Broken Heart.

In the days that followed, the valley mourned the loss of two souls Amina, taken by the violence of their world, and Zain, who had lost himself in the depths of grief.

The chinar trees stood tall and silent, bearing witness to the stories of love and loss, their leaves rustling softly in the wind as if whispering a final goodbye to the hearts that had once sought refuge beneath their branches.

Though their love had been marked by tragedy, it left an indelible mark on the valley, a testament to the resilience of the human spirit, even in the face of unimaginable heartache.

Dear Reader,

As you went through "Beneath The Chinar Trees" I eagerly await your feedback. Your thoughts and reflections are invaluable to me, whether they bring solace, tears, or simply appreciation for the journey.

I will be honoured to hear about your thinkings about this Novel…

Scan the QR Code or Visit the link to give feedback.

https://tinyurl.com/novelfeedback

www.ingramcontent.com/pod-product-compliance
Lightning Source LLC
Chambersburg PA
CBHW031256130726
47988CB00008B/3375